MW00958503

EGYPT

ANCIENT TIMES

Lori Dittmer

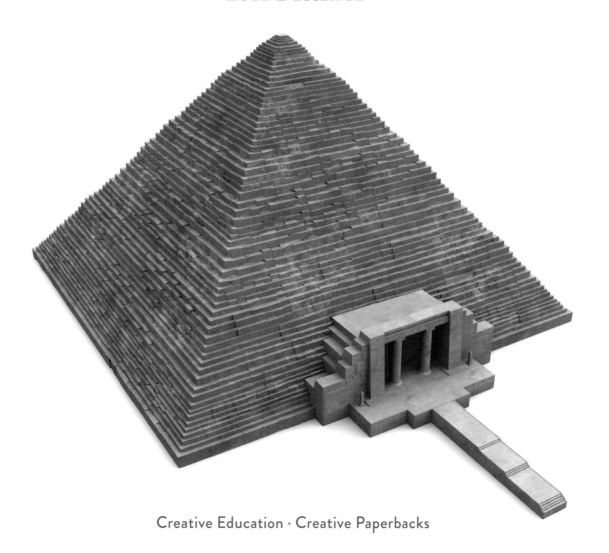

Creative Education · Creative Paperbacks

Published by Creative Education and Creative Paperbacks
P.O. Box 227, Mankato, Minnesota 56002
Creative Education and Creative Paperbacks are imprints
of The Creative Company
www.thecreativecompany.us

Design and production by Chelsey Luther
Art direction by Rita Marshall
Printed in the United States of America

Photographs by Alamy (Album, Susan Isakson, National Geographic
Image Collection), Dreamstime (Keng62fa), FreeVectorMaps.com, Getty
Images (Dorling Kindersley), National Geographic Image Collection
(WILLIAM H. BOND, H. TOM HALL, H.M. HERGET, ROBERT W. NICHOL-
SON), Shutterstock (George W. Bailey, Diospyros, Komleva, Noch, Vector
Tradition)

Copyright © 2020 Creative Education, Creative Paperbacks
International copyright reserved in all countries. No part of this book may
be reproduced in any form without written permission from the publisher.

Library of Congress Cataloging-in-Publication Data
Names: Dittmer, Lori, author.
Title: Egypt / Lori Dittmer.
Series: Ancient times.
Includes index.
Summary: This cultural overview of ancient Egypt situates the reader with-
in the society, describing key aspects of daily life, beliefs, and architectural
accomplishments such as the Great Sphinx.
Identifiers: LCCN: 2018053204 / ISBN 978-1-64026-113-6 (hardcover) / ISBN
978-1-62832-676-5 (pbk) / ISBN 978-1-64000-231-9 (eBook)
Subjects: LCSH: Egypt—Civilization—Juvenile literature.
Classification: LCC DT61 .D585 2019 / DDC 932—dc23

HC 9 8 7 6 5 4 3 2 1
PBK 9 8 7 6 5 4 3 2

CONTENTS

AFRICA

EGYPTIAN EMPIRE

Step into Ancient Egypt

Imagine you are part of an upper-class family in ancient Egypt. You have learned **hieroglyphics**, while other kids work on farms. You will spend your life preparing important documents.

TIME PERIODS OF ANCIENT EGYPT

EARLY DYNASTIC PERIOD
3100–2686 B.C.

OLD KINGDOM
2686–2181 B.C.

FIRST INTERMEDIATE PERIOD
2181–2134 B.C.

MIDDLE KINGDOM
2134–1782 B.C.

SECOND INTERMEDIATE PERIOD
1782–1550 B.C.

NEW KINGDOM
1550–1069 B.C.

THIRD INTERMEDIATE PERIOD
1069–664 B.C.

LATE DYNASTIC PERIOD
664–332 B.C.

PTOLEMAIC PERIOD
332–30 B.C.

Long ago, people settled along the Nile River in northeastern Africa. By 3100 B.C., they came together under one king. Ancient Egyptians left many artifacts behind. Today, people study these objects.

Daily Life

The pharaoh ruled ancient Egypt. Most pharaohs were men, but a few were women. When the pharaoh died, the oldest son usually took over.

Wealthy men and women bathed each day. They wore perfumed wigs. They spread makeup around their eyes. It protected them from the sun's glare.

Most people were farmers or craftspeople. They grew wheat to make bread. They made paper and baskets with **papyrus**. They celebrated when the Nile flooded. The water carried rich **silt**. This helped crops grow.

Homes were made of mud bricks. Upper-class homes had bathrooms inside. Bright murals covered the walls. Slaves worked long hours. They built pyramids and temples.

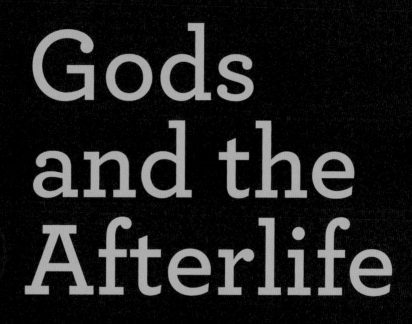

Gods and the Afterlife

Ancient Egyptians had many gods.

Ra was the sun god. He had a human

body. But he had the head of a falcon.

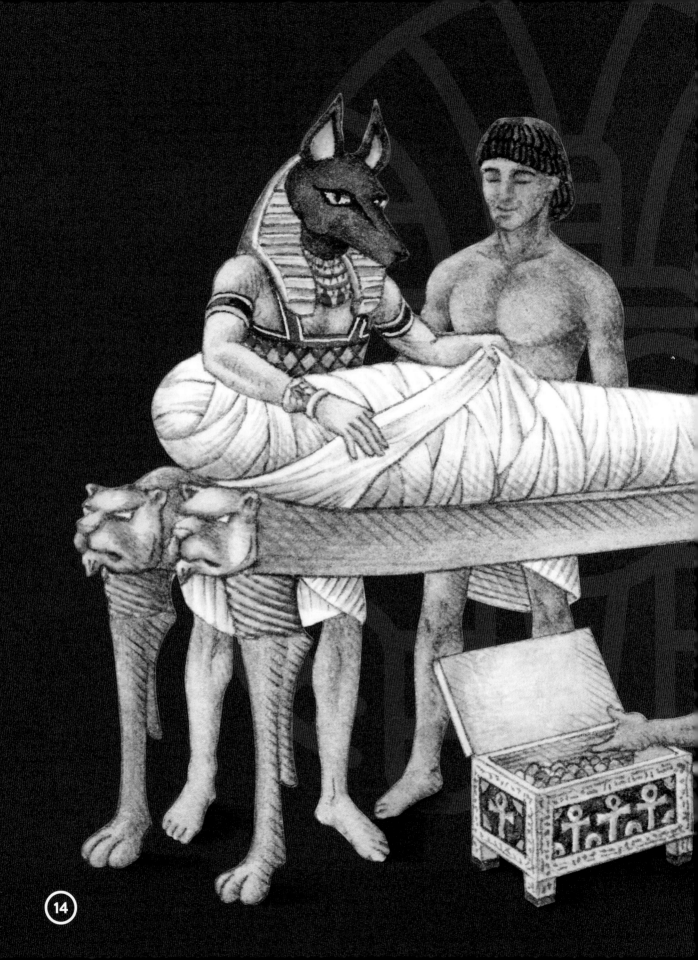

People believed that pharaohs became gods after they died. Pharaohs' bodies were **mummified**. Then they were buried in special tombs. Commoners were wrapped in cloth and buried in the desert.

The End of the Empire

By about 1000 B.C., the empire was split into several kingdoms. Cleopatra is considered the last ruler of ancient Egypt. She died in 30 B.C. Then Egypt became part of the Roman Empire.

Great Sphinx

The Great Sphinx is a statue. Carved from limestone, it has a lion's body and a human head. It is in front of the pyramids at Giza. Each year, millions of people visit the Sphinx.

ANCIENT EGYPT
TIMELINE

1479 B.C.

Hatshepsut begins her 22-year rule.

1640–1520 B.C.

A people called the Hyksos invade northern Egypt, bringing horse-drawn chariots with them.

mid–1200s B.C.

The temples at Abu Simbel are built.

3100 B.C.

Northern and southern parts unite as one Egyptian empire.

c.2900 B.C.

Papyrus becomes used as a writing material.

c.2150 B.C

Egypt splits into two countries again.

2550–2490 B.C.

The pyramids at Giza are constructed, overseen by three different kings.

332 B.C.

The Ptolemaic (Greek) Period begins with Alexander the Great's victory over Egypt.

30 B.C.

Cleopatra dies; Egypt becomes part of the Roman Empire.

Glossary

artifacts: objects made by humans long ago

hieroglyphics: a system of writing that uses pictures instead of words

mummified: preserved through a special process of drying and wrapping in cloth

murals: pictures painted on a wall

papyrus: a material made from a water plant

silt: fine bits of soil carried along in a river

Read More

Morley, Jacqueline. *You Wouldn't Want to Be a Pyramid Builder!: A Hazardous Job You'd Rather Not Have.* New York: Franklin Watts, 2014.

Raum, Elizabeth. *Egyptian Pyramids.* North Mankato, Minn.: Amicus, 2014.

Schimel, Lawrence. *If You Were a Kid Building a Pyramid.* New York: Children's Press, 2018.

Websites

DK Find Out!: Ancient Egypt
https://www.dkfindout.com/us/history/ancient-egypt/
Read more about life in ancient Egypt.

National Geographic Kids: Facts about Ancient Egypt
https://www.natgeokids.com/uk/discover/history/egypt/ten-facts-about-ancient-egypt/
Learn about the Egypt of the past and present.

Note: Every effort has been made to ensure that any websites listed above were active at the time of publication. However, because of the nature of the Internet, it is impossible to guarantee that these sites will remain active indefinitely or that their contents will not be altered.

Index

Read the entire Ancient Times series!

AZTEC
ᴇMPIRE
Lori Dittmer

CHINA
Lori Dittmer

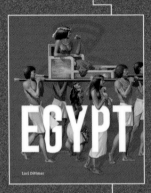

EGYPT
Lori Dittmer

GREECE
Lori Dittmer

ROME
Lori Dittmer

ATOS: 2.8
ISBN 978-1-62832-676-5   U.S. $9.99

50999

9 781628 326765

www.thecreativecompany.us

SPOTLIGHT ON NATURE
POLAR BEAR

MELISSA GISH